I0413304

# National Oceanic and Atmospheric Administration
## Office of National Marine Sanctuaries

# FINAL
## Policy and Permit guidance
## for Submarine Cable Projects

## NATIONAL OCEANIC AND ATMOSPHERIC ADMINISTRATION
## OFFICE OF NATIONAL MARINE SANCTUARIES

# FINAL
## POLICY AND PERMIT GUIDANCE
## FOR SUBMARINE CABLE PROJECTS

### PURPOSE AND APPLICATION

The purpose of this policy and permit guidance is to define and describe how the NOAA Office of National Marine Sanctuaries (ONMS) will consider proposals to install and maintain submarine cables within national marine sanctuaries.[1]

### BACKGROUND

This policy and the associated permit guidelines incorporate many lessons learned by the ONMS through direct experience with submarine cables in the Monterey Bay, Olympic Coast, and Stellwagen Bank national marine sanctuaries, as well as the experiences of other government agencies. In addition, the ONMS has taken into consideration comments received from an Advance Notice of Public Rulemaking (ANPR) regarding submarine cables in September 2000 as well as comments received in response to Interim Policy and Permit Guidance for Submarine Cable Projects (74 FR 18169; April 21, 2009). This policy statement and the associated permit guidelines reflect comments received from the ANPR and ONMS experience and information gained from previous cable projects.

### DEFINITION

For the purposes of this policy, submarine cable projects include those activities required to install and maintain cables on or in the seabed or submerged lands, including, but not limited to, cable installation (e.g., laying and burial), pre- and post-lay surveys, cable operations, maintenance and repairs, and cable removal.

### POLICY GUIDANCE

---

[1] This policy only applies to national marine sanctuaries administered under the National Marine Sanctuaries Act, 16 U.S.C. 1431-1445c.. However, due to their unique regulations, special considerations apply to the Hawaiian Islands Humpback Whale National Marine Sanctuary and the Thunder Bay National Marine Sanctuary, as described at page 10, below. In addition, this policy does not apply to the Papahanaumokuakea Marine National Monument, which is governed by other legal authorities including the Antiquities Act, 16 U.S.C. 431-433.

It is the policy of the ONMS to review applications to install and maintain submarine cables in accordance with ONMS regulations (15 CFR 922) and the guidelines provided in this document. The ONMS will approve applications for submarine cable projects only if they are found to be consistent with the criteria described in these guidelines.

# TABLE OF CONTENTS

# LIST OF APPENDICES

## LIST OF ACRONYMS

| | |
|---|---|
| AA | Assistant Administrator |
| ACOE | Army Corps of Engineers |
| ANPR | Advance Notice of Proposed Rulemaking |
| CBNMS | Cordell Bank National Marine Sanctuary |
| CINMS | Channel Islands National Marine Sanctuary |
| DOC | Department of Commerce |
| FBNMS | Fagatele Bay National Marine Sanctuary |
| FGBNMS | Flower Garden Banks National Marine Sanctuary |
| FKNMS | Florida Keys National Marine Sanctuary |
| FMV | Fair Market Value |
| GFNMS | Gulf of the Farallones National Marine Sanctuary |
| GRNMS | Gray's Reef National Marine Sanctuary |
| HIHWNMS | Hawaiian Islands Humpback Whale National Marine Sanctuary |
| MBNMS | Monterey Bay National Marine Sanctuary |
| MNMS | Monitor National Marine Sanctuary |
| NEPA | National Environmental Policy Act |
| NMSA | National Marine Sanctuaries Act |
| NMSs | National Marine Sanctuaries |
| NOAA | National Oceanic and Atmospheric Administration |
| NOS | National Ocean Service |
| OCNMS | Olympic Coast National Marine Sanctuary |
| ONMS | Office of National Marine Sanctuaries |
| SBNMS | Stellwagen Bank National Marine Sanctuary |
| SUP | Special Use Permit |
| TBNMS | Thunder Bay National Marine Sanctuary |

# 1. Introduction

The NOAA Office of National Marine Sanctuaries (ONMS) manages a system of thirteen national marine sanctuaries (NMSs or sanctuaries) that protect special, nationally significant areas of the marine environment under the authority of the National Marine Sanctuaries Act (NMSA; 16 U.S.C. 1431-1445c). Together with the U.S. Fish and Wildlife Service and the State of Hawaii, the ONMS also manages the Papahanaumokuakea Marine National Monument under the Antiquities Act, 16 U.S.C. 431-433 and Presidential Proclamation 8031. Sanctuaries and the monument protect a variety of marine habitats and cultural resources including coral reefs, mangrove forests, seagrass beds, deep-sea canyons, kelp beds, marine mammal feeding and breeding grounds, historic shipwrecks, and submerged cultural resources.

In the late 1990s, the ONMS received applications to install and maintain telecommunication submarine cables through the Olympic Coast National Marine Sanctuary (OCNMS), Stellwagen Bank National Marine Sanctuary (SBNMS), and Monterey Bay National Marine Sanctuary (MBNMS). Experience gained through the consideration and issuance of permits for those projects highlighted the need for more clarity as to how such projects would be handled in the future.

The Department of Commerce convened a workshop in February 2000 with representatives from the telecommunications and fishing industries, environmental and conservation organizations, and state agencies. A white paper with key issues and guiding principles was distributed prior to, and discussed at, the workshop. The proposed guiding principles included: analysis of habitat types appropriate or inappropriate for cable laying, analysis of individual sanctuary regulations, and parameters for evaluating proposals for cable installations.

In August 2000, NOAA published an advance notice of proposed rulemaking (ANPR) on Installing and Maintaining Commercial Submarine Cables in National Marine Sanctuaries in the Federal Register (65 FR 51264, Aug. 23, 2000). A second ANPR was published in November 2000 at the request of the industry for additional time to comment (65 FR 70537, Nov. 24, 2000). The ANPR requested comments on both the guiding principles contained in the white paper and on the issues raised at the workshop.

Specifically, the ANPR requested comments on:
- Whether changes to existing ONMS regulations or some form of policy guidance was necessary to clarify NOAA's decision-making process regarding the installation and maintenance of commercial submarine cables within NMSs;
- If changes or additional guidance were appropriate, what those changes or guidance should contain; and
- Whether there were comments on the proposed principles on the installation of commercial submarine cables within the marine and coastal environment.

The ONMS received 36 comments from the telecommunications industry, the Department of Defense, the environmental community, state government, and various interested individuals.

General comments on the ANPR included the following:
- The telecommunications industry believed that existing regulations are adequate in NMSs.
- The environmental community urged NOAA to prohibit cables within NMSs, and to develop stringent permit application criteria, including removal of out-of-service cables.
- The telecommunication industry and the environmental community did not support a Programmatic Environmental Impact Statement (PEIS) or the concept of approving projects in the planning stage.
- The environmental community supported the idea of cable corridors while the telecommunication industry opposed it.
- The telecommunication industry wanted improved consultation between NOAA and other cable permitting authorities, such as the U.S. Army Corps of Engineers, the Federal Communications Commission, and more specifically, user-friendly criteria for permit applications.

These comments, in addition to lessons learned from past direct experience related to cables installed in sanctuaries, were factors that led to NOAA's decision not to pursue rulemaking at this time, but, rather to develop and issue interim permit guidelines to apply to the installation and maintenance of cables. The ONMS believes that cable permit guidelines will ensure that applications to install and maintain submarine cables in sanctuaries are reviewed consistently and in a manner that adheres to the NMSA and ONMS regulations (15 CFR Part 922).

In 2009, the ONMS published the Interim Policy and Permit Guidance for Submarine Cable Projects (74 FR 18169 April 21, 2009. The Department of Defense (DOD) was the only entity to provide comments on the interim policy during the comment period (April 21, 2009 through May 21, 2009). However, NOAA is accepting for consideration the late-filed comments (May 28, 2009) from the North American Submarine Cable Association (NASCA), whose comments, and NOAA's responses, are judged to be generally the same as those previously published regarding the Notice of Applicability of Special Use Permit Requirements to Certain Categories of Activities Conducted Within the National Marine Sanctuary System (71 FR 4898 January 30, 2006).
The following section provides a summary of the comments received and NOAA's response:

1. *Comment*: NOAA should ensure that activities involving laying new cables and the replacement/maintenance of existing submarine cables will not be impeded (DOD).
   *Response*: Department of Defense activities are subject to sanctuary prohibitions unless they are listed as exempt military activities either at the time of sanctuary designation or as part of a rule modification.

2. *Comment:* NOAA incorrectly asserts that it definitively determined that commercial submarine cables are subject to special use permits or that special use permits are required or appropriate for undersea cables (NASCA).

*Response:* On May 20, 2002 NOAA published a revised list of categories of activities subject to special use permits (67 FR 35501) which includes the continued presence of commercial submarine cables on or beneath the seafloor as a category appropriate for special use permits.

3. *Comment:* NOAA has failed to explain the basis for its distinction between commercial and non-commercial undersea cables (NASCA).

*Response:* NOAA disagrees and is justified in making a distinction in how it processes applications to conduct activities related to cable systems for different purposes (i.e., commercial versus non-commercial cable systems). Activities related to commercial submarine cable systems do not fit within the scope of the permit types under the ONMS regulations. ONMS regulations provide for the issuance of permits for a variety of non-commercial purposes (e.g., research and education) that further a sanctuary's goals and objectives. Rather, commercial cables appear to clearly fall within the Congressional intent for the use of special use permits.

4. *Comment:* NOAA should ensure that the application of the permit guidance will not violate international law (NASCA, DOD).

*Response:* NOAA recognizes that under international law other nations are entitled to lay and maintain submarine cables on the United States' continental shelf beyond the 12-mile territorial sea. As a coastal nation, under international law the United States has sovereign rights with respect to its natural resources and may take reasonable measures to protect those resources from harmful activities, consistent with the rights of other nations under applicable international law. It is NOAA's intent to apply the NMSA and implementing regulations in a manner that both protects resources of its sanctuaries and respects the rights of other nations under international law, as is required by the NMSA.

5. *Comment:* NOAA's guidance should consider the impact on the nation's communication infrastructure (DOD).

*Response:* NOAA has added the need for the construction of a diverse, redundant national infrastructure as one of the factors it will consider under paragraph 2.2.4 of the guidance.

6. *Comment:* NOAA's guidance should not apply to national marine monuments or other areas where NOAA has management roles (DOD).

*Response:* NOAA has revised the guidance to indicate it only applies to national marine sanctuaries under the National Marine Sanctuaries Act, 16 U.S.C. 1431-1445c.

7. *Comment:* NOAA has failed to explain how its application process fits within the NEPA Framework (NASCA).

*Response:* NOAA has concluded that this permit guidance is a notice of an administrative and legal nature and will not have a significant effect, individually or cumulatively, on the human environment. As such, this action is categorically excluded from the requirement to prepare an environmental assessment or environmental impact statement in accordance with Section 6.05c3(i) of NOAA Administrative Order 216-6. Furthermore, individual permit actions by the ONMS are evaluated on a case-by-case basis. NOAA will ensure that the appropriate NEPA analysis will be completed when those actions are proposed to be taken by the ONMS prior to taking final action on a permit.

New NASCA comments:

8. *Comment:* NOAA has failed to provide for protection of proprietary and commercially-sensitive information.
   *Response:* NOAA disagrees. NOAA provides for the protection of trade secrets and commercial or financial information consistent with applicable law, including the Freedom of Information Act (5 U.S.C. 552) and implementing regulations (5 CFR Part 4).

9. *Comment:* NOAA's proposed application requirements would be extraordinarily burdensome and would violate the Paperwork Reduction Act (PRA).
   *Response:* Applications for permits discussed in this notice involve a collection-of-information requirement subject to the requirements of the PRA. OMB has approved this collection-of-information requirement under OMB control number 0648-0141 (71 FR 4902).

10. *Comment:* NOAA should refresh the record of this proceeding, as its interim guidance is based on a stale record developed more than eight years ago and otherwise based on non-public information.
    *Response:* The intent of the permit guidance is to identify the criteria the ONMS will use in reviewing permit applications for submarine cable projects proposed in national marine sanctuaries and does not preclude the submission of pertinent data by the applicant. Information supplied by the applicant, historical or new, will be considered by NOAA as part of its NEPA responsibilities for the issuance of permits.

The ONMS believes that the final cable policy and permit guidance will ensure that applications to install and maintain submarine cables in sanctuaries are reviewed consistently and in a manner that adheres to the NMSA and ONMS regulations (15 CFR Part 922).

## 2. Guidelines for Submarine Cable Permit Applications

Anyone proposing to install and maintain a submarine cable within a national marine sanctuary[2] must obtain prior approval from the ONMS via a permit or other

---

[2] See footnote 1.

authorization. It is the policy of the ONMS to review applications to install and maintain cables in accordance with the guidelines provided in this section. The intent of this section is to ensure that such applications are processed consistently throughout the ONMS. This guidance will also provide greater predictability and clarity to prospective applicants. These guidelines are to be used instead of the normal ONMS permit application forms and guidelines.[3]

The process by which applications for submarine cable permits are considered is shown in Figure 1. These guidelines explain the elements of the process in the sections indicated in the diagram.

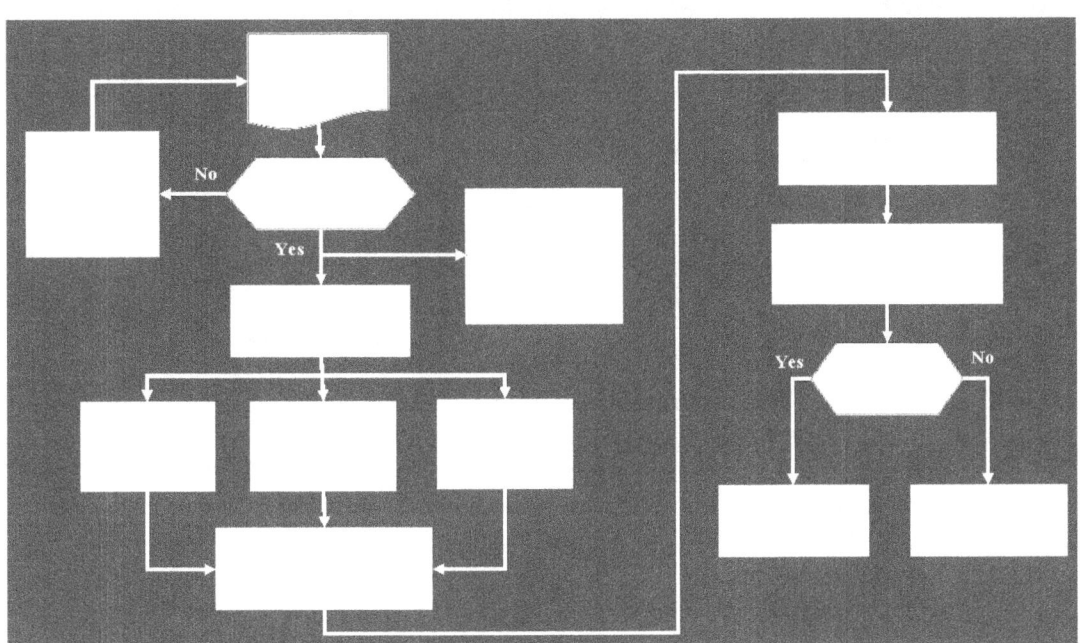

**Figure 1. ONMS cable permit application decision process**

## 2.1.    Forms of approval

In most national marine sanctuaries it is unlawful to alter or place material on the seabed or submerged lands unless conducted pursuant to a sanctuary permit or other authorization. Since cable installation activities require seabed disturbance or placement of material on the seabed, cable installation is prohibited in most sanctuaries. However, certain prohibited activities may be permitted to the extent they are compatible with the resource protection mandate of the National Marine Sanctuaries Act (NMSA) and meet the regulatory requirements for a sanctuary permit or authorization. The NMSA also provides authority to issue special use permits (SUPs) for specific activities and for the

---

[3] *"Guidelines for Submitting Applications for National Marine Sanctuary Permits and Authorizations"* available for download at http://sanctuaries.noaa.gov/management/permits/welcome.html

collection of fees for the conduct of any activity under an SUP. These forms of approval are covered in more detail beginning with section 2.1.1. Submarine cable installation and maintenance has been permitted in sanctuaries using a sanctuary regulatory permit, SUP, authorization, or combination of the three tools.

When a permit application for a submarine cable is received, the ONMS will first determine under which form of approval to consider it. As previously mentioned, cable proposals must be eligible for at least one of three primary forms of approval to be considered:

- Permits issued pursuant to site-specific regulations and 15 CFR § 922.48;
- Authorizations of other government agency approvals issued pursuant to 15 CFR § 922.49; and
- Special Use Permits issued pursuant to section 310 of the NMSA.

Because submarine cable projects can be proposed for different purposes, the appropriate form of approval for which each application should be considered will vary. In addition, not all permit types (with the exception of SUPs) are available in all sanctuaries. Applicants should consult 15 CFR Part 922 for the applicable ONMS regulations or contact the appropriate sanctuary superintendent regarding permit types for that sanctuary.

This policy guidance does not apply to the Hawaiian Islands Humpback Whale National Marine Sanctuary (HIHWNMS) or the Thunder Bay National Marine Sanctuary (TBNMS). In HIHWNMS, activities involving alteration of the seabed or placement of material on it are lawful if conducted pursuant to a valid federal or state permit. In TBNMS, activities involving the lake bottom are lawful except in areas of lake bottom associated with underwater cultural resources. However, in all national marine sanctuaries, including HIHWNMS and TBNMS, if another Federal permit or license is required to install such cables, the Federal agency issuing such permit is required to first consult with the ONMS in accordance with section 304(d) of the NMSA.[4]

ONMS staff will review all applications for completeness and consistency with these guidelines. The ONMS may hire an independent consultant or consult with other subject matter experts to assist in the administration of the technical review of the permit application. If a project does not qualify for one of these three forms of approval (permit, authorization, or special use permit) the project will not be reviewed further in accordance with these guidelines. These applications will either be denied without additional review or returned to the applicant.

---

[4] Section 304(d) of the National Marine Sanctuaries Act (16 U.S.C. § 1434(d)) requires Federal agencies to consult with ONMS prior to taking any action likely to destroy, cause the loss of, or injure any sanctuary resource (for SBNMS, the threshold is any action that "may affect" sanctuary resources). Moreover, if a Federal agency takes an action other than the alternative recommended by the ONMS, resulting in the destruction of, loss of, or injury to a sanctuary resource, that agency is required to promptly prevent and mitigate further damage and restore or replace the sanctuary resource in a manner approved by the Secretary of Commerce. 16 U.S.C.§ 1434(d).

2.1.1. Permits

Most sanctuaries have regulations that allow permits to be issued for activities that would otherwise be prohibited when those activities are related to research, education, or management. Additional permit categories are available for Indian tribal welfare (Olympic Coast National Marine Sanctuary) and for furthering sanctuary purposes (Florida Keys National Marine Sanctuary). These permit categories are included here because they could potentially allow installation and maintenance of submarine cables at these two sanctuaries. In order to qualify for a regulatory sanctuary permit, a cable project must meet the description of these permit types, which are described in more detail below.[5]

*Research*

In order to qualify for a research permit a submarine cable project should further research related to sanctuary resources and qualities. Installation of cables should be part of a scientific research project that would answer scientific questions about sanctuary resources. However, research questions with little or no applicability to sanctuary management goals (i.e., the information it expects to yield is either widely known or inconsequential to sanctuary management) would not likely be approved. This permit type is available at all sanctuaries.

*Education*

In order to qualify for an education permit a cable project should be part of an educational project that would increase the awareness of sanctuary users about the sanctuary or a particular aspect of the sanctuary, as opposed to simply increasing awareness or understanding about submarine cables. In addition, an educational project involving the placement of submarine cables must be conducted in a manner or in a location where a reasonable number of sanctuary users will be able to benefit from its presence. Education permits are available for all sanctuaries except the *Monitor* NMS.

*Management*

In order to qualify as a management permit a submarine cable project should assist NOAA in managing the sanctuary. Applicability of any particular cable project to this type of permit is dependent upon the management goals outlined in sanctuary-specific management plans. A cable project should be reasonably expected to help the sanctuary meet a previously stated management goal to qualify for this permit type. The sanctuary will not create new management objectives (i.e., management objectives not articulated in the sanctuary's management plan) simply so that a proposed cable project might qualify for this permit type. This permit type is available at all sanctuaries except: Fagatele Bay, Gray's Reef, Hawaiian Islands Humpback Whale, *Monitor* and Thunder Bay.

---

[5] Other regulatory permit types were omitted because they would not reasonably apply to submarine cable projects (e.g., permits for "conduct general salvage and recovery operations" or "removal of jade").

*Furthering the welfare of an Indian tribe adjacent to the sanctuary – Olympic Coast National Marine Sanctuary (OCNMS) only*

OCNMS regulations allow for the issuance of a permit for an activity that would otherwise be prohibited if it would promote the welfare of a federally-recognized Native American tribe with treaty rights within the sanctuary. A proposed change to these regulations (76 FR 2611; January 14, 2011) would clarify the permit to allow otherwise prohibited activities if they promote or enhance tribal self-determination, tribal government functions, the exercise of treaty rights, the economic development of the tribe, subsistence, ceremonial and spiritual activities, and/or the education or training of tribal members of American Indian tribes adjacent to the sanctuary (i.e., Hoh, Makah, and Quileute Tribes and the Quinault Indian Nation) or its designee. These permit criteria are consistent with Executive Order 13175 on Consultation and Coordination with Indian Tribal Governments.

*Otherwise further Sanctuary purposes – Florida Keys National Marine Sanctuary (FKNMS) only*

FKNMS regulations (15 CFR § 922.166(2)(vi)) allow the ONMS to permit prohibited activities that "otherwise further the [FKNMS] purposes, including facilitating multiple use of the [FKNMS], to the extent compatible with the primary objective of resource protection." The purposes of the FKNMS are as follows:

- To protect, preserve and manage the conservation, ecological, recreational, research, educational, historical, and aesthetic resources and qualities of the area,
- To protect, restore, and enhance the living resources of the Sanctuary,
- To contribute to the maintenance of natural assemblages of living resources for future generations,
- To provide places for species dependent on such living resources to survive and propagate,
- To facilitate to the extent compatible with the primary objective of resource protection all public and private uses of the resources of the Sanctuary not prohibited pursuant to other authorities,
- To reduce conflicts between such compatible uses, and
- To achieve the other policies and purposes of the Florida Keys National Marine Sanctuary and Protection Act and the National Marine Sanctuaries Act.

If a cable project would further one of these purposes, it would be eligible for consideration within FKNMS under this permit category.

## 2.1.2. Authorizations

In certain sanctuaries a sanctuary superintendent can also authorize an otherwise prohibited activity if that activity is permitted by a valid lease, permit, license, approval or other authorization issued by any federal, state, or local authority of competent jurisdiction. Such approval by the sanctuary superintendent is known as an "authorization." Since the general process and requirements governing the handling of authorizations and permits are similar, in these guidelines the term "permit" applies to both permits and authorizations. When there is a difference in the requirements or process between permits and authorizations, this distinction is noted. The authority to issue authorizations is limited to the following sanctuaries: Florida Keys, Flower Garden Banks, Monterey Bay, Stellwagen Bank, Olympic Coast, and Thunder Bay. In those sites where it is an option, authorization authority would typically be used in cases where a regulatory sanctuary permit is not available.

To initiate the authorization process, applicants must notify the sanctuary superintendent of their desire to use another agency's permit to conduct an otherwise prohibited activity in the sanctuary. The ONMS will then notify the applicant and permitting agency as to whether it objects to the issuance of the agency permit. If the ONMS does not object, it will authorize, in writing, the use of the other permit, which will allow the activity to be conducted lawfully in the sanctuary. This authorization will resemble a permit and generally contain additional conditions on the conduct of the activity deemed necessary to protect sanctuary resources and qualities. If the ONMS objects to the other agency permit, or otherwise does not provide written authorization, the activity may not be conducted in the sanctuary.

Most cable projects will require a permit from the U.S. Army Corps of Engineers (ACOE) pursuant to the ACOE's authority under Section 10 of the Rivers and Harbors Act or Section 404 of the Clean Water Act. If the ONMS decides to authorize another agency's permit (rather than issue a sanctuary permit), a permit from the ACOE would be a likely vehicle through which the ONMS could authorize cable projects in cases where a permit or a special use permit is not available.

## 2.1.3 Special use permits

Special use permits are issued pursuant to Section 310 of the NMSA (16 U.S.C. §1441), which allows issuance of special use permits for specific activities in a sanctuary only if such authorization is necessary: (1) to establish conditions of access to and use of any sanctuary resource; or (2) to promote public use and understanding of a sanctuary resource. Activities that are necessary to establish conditions of access to and use of sanctuary resources generally have included concessionaire-type activities (profit-driven entities operating within the boundaries of a national marine sanctuary and other commercial activities that require access to the sanctuary to achieve a desired goal). Special use permits can be issued for any sanctuary.

The NMSA (16 U.S.C. § 1441(c)) requires that special use permits:
- Authorize the conduct of an activity only if that activity is compatible with the purposes for which the Sanctuary is designated and with protection of Sanctuary resources;
- Not authorize the conduct of any activity for a period of more than five years unless renewed;
- Require that activities carried out under the permit be conducted in a manner that does not destroy, cause the loss of, or injure sanctuary resources; and

- Require the permittee to purchase and maintain comprehensive general liability insurance, or post an equivalent bond, against claims arising out of activities conducted under the permit and agree to hold the United States harmless against such claims.

Should the ONMS determine that a special use permit is appropriate for the continued presence and operation of a specific submarine cable project, it will process the application consistent with Section 310 of the NMSA in addition to these guidelines. Clarification on the applicability of SUP requirements to certain categories of activities conducted within national marine sanctuaries was described in a Final Notice in the Federal Register in January 2006 (71 FR 4898, January 30, 2006).[6] The notice specifies that the continued presence of commercial submarine cables beneath or on the seabed will be subject to the requirements of special use permits under Section 310 of the NMSA.

For special use permits only, the ONMS has the authority to recoup an application fee for processing the permit, the administrative cost of ongoing monitoring of the permit, and the fair market value (FMV) of the use of sanctuary resources. The ONMS has developed a process for determining the FMV of special use permits issued for the presence of submarine cables. The final report of that analysis, "Fair Market Value Analysis for Fiber Optic Cable Permit in National Marine Sanctuaries," presents the methodology by which the ONMS will assess the FMV for the presence of any future commercial submarine cable in a national marine sanctuary.[7] The notice of the availability of the FMV analysis report was published in the Federal Register in August 2002 (67 FR 55201, August 28, 2002). The FMV process described in the analysis was based on dozens of industry and government sources and draws on collaboration with and review by numerous business, legal, and technical experts. The ONMS has issued two special use permits allowing the presence of commercial submarine cables in national marine sanctuaries, one each in Olympic Coast and Stellwagen Bank sanctuaries.

## 2.2. Regulatory Review Criteria

Once the form of approval (permit, special use permit, or authorization) under which the application will be considered is determined, the ONMS will evaluate applications for the installation and maintenance of submarine cables based on the criteria listed below. As a matter of policy, these criteria will be applied to every application regardless of the form of approval selected.

ONMS regulations provide review criteria by which office staff must evaluate permit applications. This document combines those criteria into four categories. First, the ONMS will conduct a technical review of the methods proposed to install and maintain

---

[6] The Federal Register Notice is available for download at
http://sanctuaries.noaa.gov/management/fr/71_fr_4898.pdf
[7] The report "A Fair Market Value Analysis for Submarine Cable Permit in National Marine Sanctuaries" is available for download at http://sanctuaries.noaa.gov/library/national/fmvfinalreport.pdf

the submarine cable(s). Next, the ONMS will evaluate the impacts of the proposed submarine cable on sanctuary resources. The ONMS will then consider the proposed benefits of the project. Finally, the ONMS will consider other matters important for the review of cable projects that are not specifically provided in the ONMS regulations.

## 2.2.1. Technical Review

The following criteria apply to the review of the project itself. Under these criteria the ONMS considers the applicant's qualifications and financial resources, the methods proposed by the applicant to install and maintain the cable, and the route the applicant has chosen.

*Professional and financial responsibility*

The professional and financial responsibility of an applicant proposing to install a submarine cable must be demonstrated prior to ONMS approving such activity. The ONMS will first review the qualifications of the individual or entity proposing to install a submarine cable in a sanctuary. The ONMS will use the following questions to evaluate an applicant's qualifications:
- Does the applicant have the technical skills to install and maintain a submarine cable consistent with all applicable permit conditions?
- Will the applicant be able to fulfill any permit requirements established to minimize or eliminate impacts to sanctuary resources?

For example, if an applicant claims to be able to install a submarine cable in a precise corridor, the ONMS must ensure that the applicant has the skills and equipment available to do this. To ensure that an applicant has the technical skills to comply with a permit to install, maintain, and monitor a submarine cable, the ONMS will request that the applicant submit professional qualifications as stated in the permit guidelines in Appendix B for each of those involved in the project installation and maintenance. The ONMS will not likely approve projects that rely on inexperienced persons to perform activities related to the installation and monitoring of a submarine cable when those activities are critical to the project's compliance with permit terms and conditions.

The financial responsibility in many cases relates to both the applicant's budget for the activity as well as the financial resources of the applicant to comply with the terms and conditions of any permit. The following questions will help the ONMS determine if an applicant can exercise appropriate financial responsibility for the proposed project:
- Can the applicant show that adequate funds are available to remove or remediate the cable if something were to go wrong during or after installation?
- Can the applicant show that there are funds available to comply with permit terms and conditions for the life of the project, including any monitoring programs and cable removal requirements?

Projects that involve the installation and maintenance of cables should include plans and documentation of sufficient funding to remove the cable after the project is finished. Lack of adequate funding to remove the cable is not sufficient justification to avoid cable removal. (Refer to *Permit Terms and Conditions (p. 23)* for information on bonding and insurance requirements). Applicants proposing projects involving cables that need to be in place long-term should be able to sufficiently justify that the length of time is necessary to meet the objectives of the project. In some cases the impacts of cable removal will be greater than leaving it in place. In these cases, the ONMS may consider allowing the cable to remain in the sanctuary permanently, although this will be evaluated initially before the cable is installed and will factor into the decision to permit the cable in the first place.

To ensure that funds are available for the life of a project, the ONMS will require the applicant to post a performance bond or equivalent financial assurance to ensure that permit terms and conditions will be met for the life of the project. This includes, but is not limited to, any requirements for cable removal and long-term monitoring.

*Appropriateness of methods*

The ONMS will also consider the appropriateness of the methods a permit applicant is proposing to use for cable installation and project maintenance. The ONMS will rely on past experience, sanctuary staff experience, and expert advice to ensure that more efficient, less costly, or less damaging methods available to achieve the project goals have not been overlooked. Different methods of installing cables may be appropriate in different sanctuaries or in different habitats within a single sanctuary. The following will be considered to determine if the proposed methods are appropriate:

- The applicant should demonstrate why the proposed method was chosen and why it was deemed superior to other methods not selected.
- If the applicant has dismissed alternative methods that impact sanctuary resources to a lesser degree (as compared to the proposal), the applicant must provide a thorough justification.
- An applicant's lack of funds to pursue an alternative method is not, by itself, a justification for rejecting an alternative that the ONMS determines to be less damaging to sanctuary resources.

Under this criterion the ONMS will also carefully evaluate the method for installing and maintaining the cables. Appendix B discusses the information required from the applicant in order for the ONMS to make this assessment. As described in more detail in the appendix, applicants should include in their application a description of how these issues will be addressed by their project by providing the following:

- A detailed description of the cable route; information on construction, operations, and abandonment; and emergency response resources and capability;
- A monitoring plan for both installation and long-term placement that includes components addressing biological effects, effectiveness in meeting stated goals, and bonding/financial assurance; and
- An analysis of the environmental consequences of installation and long-term placement that includes details about the affected environment and the potential adverse and beneficial effects of the project.

As part of its responsibilities under this criterion and to comply with the National Environmental Policy Act (NEPA) (see section 2.4.1), the ONMS may ask the applicant to investigate and analyze other methods that can be reasonably expected to achieve the stated goals of the project. One of the alternatives the ONMS may require the applicant to investigate and analyze is one that does not involve the placement of any material on the seafloor or submerged lands (i.e., meet the project purpose without installing a cable). The ONMS may also require the applicant to provide a written analysis of other alternative methodologies. Related to this, the ONMS will also require the applicant to justify the site selected for the proposal and analyze alternative sites that can be expected to achieve the stated goals of the project, including sites outside the sanctuary.

*Activity needs to be in a sanctuary*

As stated previously, the installation of submarine cables in sanctuaries is prohibited except where permitted. A proponent of a cable project must justify to the ONMS that the cable needs to be located inside the sanctuary to achieve the stated goals.

To satisfy this criterion and a portion of the ONMS's obligations under NEPA, applicants for approvals to install a cable in a sanctuary should:
- Provide an analysis that compares the environmental impacts of the in-sanctuary proposal to at least one non-sanctuary alternative site;
- Explain why the in-sanctuary proposal is preferable to locating the project outside the sanctuary in terms of providing greater benefits; and
- Provide the siting criteria that led to the conclusion that the site within the sanctuary is the only one that meets the project's goals.

If any non-sanctuary alternative (either one analyzed by the applicant or another analyzed by the ONMS) can reasonably be expected to achieve the desired goals of the project, the application is not likely to be approved.

2.2.2. Evaluating the effects of the project

The following four criteria are used to evaluate the potential effects of proposed submarine cable projects and evaluate the significance of those effects. These effects will be evaluated in detail in the NEPA analysis described in section 2.4.1. Although they are among the most important criteria the ONMS will consider, they can usually be evaluated more effectively after the ONMS has completed its initial review of the project as described in section 2.2.1.

Because the long-term effects of submarine cable installation and long-term placement are not well understood, the applicant will generally be required to conduct or fund a long-term monitoring project. Refer to section 2.5.1 for details on monitoring requirements.

*Extent to which the activity will diminish or enhance the values of the sanctuary*

Key components of the review of proposed submarine cable projects is the determination of whether the project is compatible with the primary resource protection mandate of the

NMSA and determining whether the proposed benefits of the project to the sanctuary outweigh the potential adverse impacts to sanctuary resources and values. When processing submarine cable permit applications, the ONMS will consider the extent to which a proposed project is expected to affect the values for which the applicable sanctuary was designated. The following are the primary values of sanctuaries that will be considered under this criterion (as they relate to the installation of cables) along with questions that will help assess how each value is affected. Because the primary reason for which sanctuaries are designated is the protection of sanctuary resources, the effects of a project on these resources are given the most weight:

1. Natural and cultural resource protection value:
   - How does the project enhance or diminish the protection of the natural and cultural resources in the sanctuary?
   - What are the long-term and short-term impacts to sanctuary resources and values? Will those impacts be significant?
   - What natural communities can the ONMS reasonably expect to be displaced when the submarine cable is installed?
   - Will the installation and operation of the submarine cable inhibit the management or protection of a cultural resource site?
2. Value of the site as a source for scientific and educational information:
   - How does the project affect on-going or potential scientific monitoring projects?
   - Will the project enhance the ONMS's understanding of its resources?
   - Will the project enhance sanctuary users' knowledge about sanctuary resources?
3. Aesthetic value of the site:
   - How does the project diminish or enhance the aesthetics of the sanctuary?
   - Will the project have visual impacts?
4. Human use value:
   - How does the project diminish or enhance (on a temporary, long-term, or permanent basis) the conduct of typical human use activities at the site?
   - Will the submarine cable create new conflicts between different user groups?
   - Will the cable create a hazard to navigation?
   - What is the expected distribution of economic impacts; will the project have localized effects in communities or the adjoining region?

Under this criterion, the ONMS will consider both the positive and negative effects of a submarine cable project on these values.

*Duration of activity and effects*

The ONMS will consider the duration of a submarine cable project when evaluating each project. As a general rule, cables will be required to be removed at the end of the project.

The ONMS will also evaluate the duration of the effects of a submarine cable project before issuing a permit. A project whose adverse effects continue beyond the installation phase would have less chance of being permitted than a project whose adverse effects occur primarily during installation.

*Cumulative Impacts*

As part of its evaluation of the effects of each cable project, the ONMS will consider the cumulative impacts of the project before making a decision. The ONMS will evaluate cumulative effects consistent with the Council on Environmental Quality's implementing regulations for NEPA and its publication entitled *Considering Cumulative Effects under the National Environmental Policy Act.*[8] To facilitate this analysis, as part of the application package the applicant should:

1. Identify all natural resources (fish, benthic invertebrates, marine mammals, etc.), cultural resources (prehistoric archeological sites, historic shipwrecks, etc.), and current human uses (fishing, diving, etc.) that could potentially be affected, both positively and negatively, by the submarine cable project;
2. Identify and describe the geographic and temporal range of all affected resources;
3. Analyze how the project will affect all resources identified;
4. Describe all other natural and human-caused effects (both adverse and beneficial) on all resources identified (e.g., fishing, shipwrecks, and other cables); and
5. Describe how/if the proposed cable project will interact with the other natural and human-caused effects on the resources.

The ONMS will require a comparable level of analysis for each alternative. This criterion may result in ONMS denying a permit application due to the cumulative impacts of other projects combined, rather than solely the impacts of the proposed project.

*Impacts on adjacent Indian tribes*

The ONMS will consider the impacts of a proposed submarine cable project on federally recognized Native American tribes with treaty rights within the sanctuary. This is particularly important for projects proposed in the Olympic Coast National Marine Sanctuary (OCNMS), where staff has developed a consultation procedure with the tribes to make this determination. If a tribe objects to the installation of the submarine cable based on expected impacts to them or their activities, the ONMS will consider the objection in the review of the application.

2.2.3. Considering the end value of the activity to the sanctuary

Once the impacts of a submarine cable project have been evaluated (section 2.2.2), the ONMS will measure those impacts against the expected benefits, or "end value," of the project to the sanctuary. The nature of the end value of a project may result in the ONMS approving a submarine cable project despite the environmental impacts that may result. In general, activities that have a positive end value to the sanctuaries will have a

---

[8] See http://ceq.hss.doe.gov/publications/cumulative_effects.html for the text of this publication. CEQ regulations define cumulative impact as the impacts on the environment that result from the incremental impact of the action when added to other past, present, and reasonably foreseeable future actions. Cumulative impacts can result from individually minor but collectively significant actions taking place over a period of time.

favorable rating under this criterion, whereas those that are expected to result in little or no end value to the sanctuaries will not. The end value of any cable project can be assessed by answering the questions:

- What benefits will the sanctuary gain by this cable being installed as proposed?
- How do these benefits compare to the benefits of the submarine cable not being installed and the overall impact on sanctuary resources and qualities?
- How would the project impact local and regional economies, and how would that impact the sanctuary?

### 2.2.4. Considering other matters deemed appropriate

In some cases, the ONMS would consider other factors not presented above to determine whether or not to approve a particular submarine cable project. For example, in making its decision, the ONMS would consider the socioeconomic effects of a submarine cable project, the human safety concerns, and homeland security issues that may result from a project. While these considerations are not specified in review decision criteria in ONMS regulations or part of the ONMS's legislative mandate, they may factor into decisions in some cases when these effects are considered to be significant. While socioeconomic factors by themselves are not likely to result in the denial or approval of a permit, they may result in the addition of certain permit conditions to minimize the adverse effects.

### 2.3.  Regulatory Thresholds

ONMS regulations bar the issuance of permits in some sanctuaries for activities that exceed certain specified thresholds of impact. The ONMS cannot approve applications for permits in Fagatele Bay (FBNMS), Monterey Bay (MBNMS), Stellwagen Bank (SBNMS), and Olympic Coast (OCNMS) national marine sanctuaries if the proposed activity exceeds the threshold applicable to the sanctuary, as described below.

FBNMS has two thresholds that apply: (1) permitted activities cannot cause long-term or irreparable harm to sanctuary resources and must be conducted with adequate safeguards for the environment; and (2) the environment, after the completion of the project, will be returned to, or will regenerate to, the condition that existed before the activity occurred. MBNMS and SBNMS regulations both prohibit the issuance of permits for activities with impacts on sanctuary resources that are greater than short-term and negligible. Finally, the ONMS cannot issue a permit for an activity in OCNMS if it would substantially injure sanctuary resources and qualities. These thresholds of impact will be evaluated through the NEPA analysis process described in section 2.4.

### 2.4.  Statutory Compliance and Interagency Consultation

When permitting submarine cables, the ONMS must comply with all other applicable Federal laws. These include but are not limited to the National Environmental Policy Act (NEPA) 42 U.S.C Section 4321 et.seq.; Section 106 of the National Historic Preservation Act; Section 7 of the Endangered Species Act; the Essential Fish Habitat provisions of the Magnuson-Stevens Act; and the Federal consistency provisions of the Coastal Zone Management Act.

In most cases, required consultations and environmental documentation must be completed before the ONMS can issue a permit or authorization for a submarine cable. If the project requires an environmental assessment or environmental impact statement to comply with NEPA, completing these requirements can add significant processing time to making the decision on an application. The information included by the applicant as part of a complete application will assist the ONMS in completing its NEPA responsibilities.

## 2.5. Taking Final Action on the Permit Application

The ONMS will make a decision on a pending permit application to install a submarine cable only after it has determined the appropriate form of approval as outlined in section 2.1, has considered all of the permitting review criteria and thresholds listed and described in sections 2.2 and 2.3 respectively, and prepared the appropriate NEPA documentation and conducted all of the interagency consultations described in section 2.4. Once a decision has been reached in this manner, the ONMS will adhere to the following procedures for issuance of the permit or denial, whichever the case may be. For the most part, the ONMS will do this in the same manner as all other permit applications consistent with long-standing protocols and permit processing procedures (and national policies).

Applicants also have the right to appeal ONMS decisions on permit applications. The procedures for appeal are summarized in section 2.5.3 and are detailed in 15 CFR § 922.50.

### 2.5.1. Permit Issuance

If ONMS decides to issue a permit, it will draft the permit with all necessary special and general conditions at the sanctuary in which the submarine cable is to be installed. In addition to the typical general conditions attached to all ONMS permits and authorizations, the items described in the subsections below will be addressed in every approval to install a submarine cable as terms or conditions of the approval.

As a general rule, the ONMS will provide the applicant with an opportunity to review the draft permit. If the applicant has questions or desires clarifications or changes to the permit language, it should raise them at this time. The ONMS is under no obligation to modify the draft permit, but will work with the applicant to clarify language and make changes to which it has no objection. The applicant is required to countersign the permit and return any originals as directed by the permit before beginning any activities allowed under the permit.

*Monitoring Requirements*

An applicant who is granted a permit for a submarine cable project in a sanctuary will generally be required as a condition of that approval to fund or conduct several types of monitoring. These monitoring requirements will be included as conditions in the permit.

Monitoring typically required for approved submarine cable permits includes:
- Marine mammal monitoring (to include observers, safety zones, suspension procedures, and reports) during project installation and construction.
- Post-installation cable monitoring for the life of the cable, to include periodic cable route surveys, impact analyses, assessment of cable compared to the "as-built" plan, and reports.
- Other monitoring deemed necessary to protect sanctuary resources and qualities over the life of the project.

The ONMS will review proposed monitoring plans as part of the overall proposal. In addition, the permit will generally specify that certain plans must be approved by the ONMS before some activities relating to cable operations can take place. The applicant must show that funds or resources for the monitoring program will be available for the permit duration. As stated in section 2.2.1 of these guidelines, the ONMS will require a permittee to post a performance bond or equivalent financial assurance to ensure that permit conditions, such as long-term monitoring and cable removal requirements, can be met. This will ensure that any required monitoring will be completed even if a permittee becomes unable to fund or conduct it themselves. Proof of assurance will be required before activities under the permit will be allowed to occur.

*Permit Terms and Conditions*

Permits for cable projects may include any terms and conditions deemed necessary to adequately protect and manage sanctuary resources. The specific terms and conditions will necessarily vary from project to project. Project-specific terms and conditions may be in addition to the standard general conditions required of all sanctuary permits. Schedules of the monitoring, reporting and notification requirements will be specified in the terms and conditions. These conditions may generally include, but are not limited to, the following:

1. Cable installation requirements and procedures, including the entity and vessel-type to conduct the installation, NOAA observer coverage, weather restrictions, required cable burial depth, specifications for burial in different seabed types, prohibition on cable loops, and speed restrictions for vessel operations.
2. Any pre-installation survey requirements, such as pre-lay multi-beam sonar and grapple runs along the cable route.
3. Details of any monitoring or mitigation plans determined necessary to protect sanctuary resources and qualities, including required elements, schedules, and notifications.
4. Spill control measures, including development of a spill prevention and control and countermeasure plan ("spill plan") and a drill fluid monitoring and remediation plan for any horizontal directional drilling activities.

5. Archeological resources assessment and procedures, including review of the cable corridor for historical resources and procedures to be followed if archeological resources are discovered during the conduct of permitted activities.
6. Any required notifications to affected sanctuary offices and other personnel or agencies.
7. Vessel operations requirements, including procedures for notification of vessels and the US Coast Guard of permitted activities, mitigations required to minimize marine bird collisions due to project lighting, and regulations of vessel discharge.
8. Coordination with fishermen or fishing organizations affected by the cable project, which may include reimbursement to fishermen.
9. Procedures to be taken in event of a marine mammal or fishing gear entanglement.
10. Requirement for certain post-lay inspection and burial surveys, data, and reports, which may include a Post-Lay Inspection and Burial (PLIB) survey, raw georeferenced data from the PLIB survey, PLIB report from the survey, and updates to NOAA navigation charts.
11. When the permitted activities include placement of scientific equipment, requirements for requests for new equipment as well as procedures governing the removal and retrieval of equipment.
12. Development and implementation of cable monitoring and survey plans covering the life of the cable, to include survey types, frequency, ROV and observer coverage, cable tracking system technology requirements, mitigation measures in case of unanticipated impacts to sanctuary resources, and a cable reburial plan.
13. Cable repair procedures, including any required plans, notifications, approvals, and post-repair reports.
14. Procedures governing removal of the cable, including development and approval of a cable removal plan.
15. Bonding and insurance requirements covering the conduct of activities under the permit, to include any required monitoring or removal of the cable and associated structures.
16. For cable projects authorized under special use permits, the amounts and payment schedule for fees associated with processing and administering the permit as well as the fair market value of the use of sanctuary resources.

2.5.2. Permit Denial

If ONMS denies an application, it will promptly notify the applicant via regular and electronic mail and make available the final NEPA document supporting this decision (if one was prepared). The ONMS may provide the applicant or other Federal, state, and local agencies involved with the proposal advance notice of a pending denial in order to solicit comment on that determination.

2.5.3. Appeals

ONMS regulations at 15 CFR § 922.50 allow permit applicants to appeal a decision made by the ONMS and explain the process to make an appeal. Appellants must make their appeal in writing and submit it to the Assistant Administrator for the National Ocean Service (AA). The AA may then request additional information if he/she deems such information necessary to process the appeal. The AA will decide if an informal administrative hearing is warranted. For the Monitor sanctuary, hearings must be granted if requested. If warranted, the AA will appoint an officer to hear the case who will make a recommendation to the AA after the hearing is closed. The AA will then decide the appeal based on: (1) the regulatory requirements by which the ONMS made the initial decision, (2) the record before the ONMS available at the time the decision was made, as augmented by the AA, and (3) the record of the administrative hearing (if one was held).

# APPENDIX A:
## PERMITS ISSUED FOR SUBMARINE CABLES IN NATIONAL MARINE SANCTUARIES

| Cable/Project Title | Sanctuary | Permit Number | Permit Type | Current Permittee | # Cables | Year Installed | Comment |
|---|---|---|---|---|---|---|---|
| Monterey Accelerated Research System (MARS) Cabled Observatory | Monterey Bay | MBNMS-2002-039 | Research | Monterey Bay Aquarium Research Institute | 1 | 2007 | |
| Hibernia Transatlantic Telecommunications Project | Stellwagen Bank | SBNMS-2000-001 | Authorization/ Special Use Permit | Hibernia Atlantic | 1 | 2000 | Former permittee: 360networks |
| Pacific Crossing (PC-1) | Olympic Coast | OCNMS-2005-013 | Authorization/ Special Use Permit | PC Landing Corp. and Tyco Telecommunications (US) Inc. | 2 | 1999 | Replaced permit OCNMS-1999-001. Former permitee: Global Crossing |
| Alaska United | Olympic Coast | OCNMS-16-98 | Authorization | Alaska United Fiber System Partnership | 1 | 1998 | |
| Acoustic Thermometry of Ocean Climate (ATOC) Cable at Pioneer Seamount | Monterey Bay | MBNMS-2001-031 | Research | NOAA Office of Atmospheric Research (OAR) | 1 | 1995 | Replaced permit MBNMS-1995-012. Former permitee: Scripps Institute of Technology |

# APPENDIX B:
## PERMIT APPLICATION REQUIREMENTS FOR
## SUBMARINE CABLES IN NATIONAL MARINE SANCTUARIES[9]

### GENERAL GUIDANCE

### Background
The National Marine Sanctuaries Act (16 U.S.C. § 1431 *et seq.*) directs the Secretary of Commerce to designate and manage areas of the marine environment with nationally significant aesthetic, ecological, historical, or recreational values as national marine sanctuaries. The Office of National Marine Sanctuaries (ONMS) has issued regulations to implement this act, safeguard resources within sanctuary boundaries, and prohibit the conduct of some activities. Program regulations (15 CFR Part 922) also outline the procedure and criteria under which the ONMS will issue permits to allow certain activities that would otherwise be prohibited.

These guidelines describe the process and requirements by which an applicant may apply for a permit under this authority to install and maintain a submarine cable in a national marine sanctuary.

Anyone conducting prohibited activities without a valid national marine sanctuary permit may be subject to the penalties as provided under Section 307 of the National Marine Sanctuaries Act.

### When do I use this guidance?
Applications should follow the format given in this guidance whenever an individual or organization wishes to install a submarine cable in or through a national marine sanctuary.

### How do I apply? Is there an application form?
Due to the complex and (generally) extensive nature of the information required, there is no permit application form that must be completed for submarine cable applications. The applicant should instead develop an application "package" that includes all the information required by these guidelines. The applicant has wide latitude to decide what this package looks like, so long as it is well organized and contains all the required elements. A complete application package need not take the form of a single file or document.

### When should I apply?
Permit applications should be submitted at least six (6) months in advance of the requested effective date to allow sufficient time for evaluation and processing. However, since applications for submarine cables can take up a year to process (due to required compliance with other laws, such as the National Environmental Policy Act), submissions of applications as far in advance as possible are encouraged.

In order to expedite processing, applicants are encouraged to contact the appropriate sanctuary superintendent in advance of submitting a formal application to discuss any questions or issues

---

[9] See discussion at page 10 regarding the circumstances applicable to submarine cables installed in the Hawaiian Islands Humpback Whale National Marine Sanctuary and Thunder Bay National Marine Sanctuary.

they feel may complicate or delay the application process. Applications not received within the time frames specified above are not guaranteed to be processed before the requested effective date.

**Where do I apply?**

A complete permit application package and any supplemental materials should be submitted to the office for the sanctuary in which you plan to install the submarine cable. For activities proposed in more than one sanctuary, a "lead" sanctuary is usually designated to handle the application. If in doubt, contact the ONMS national permit coordinator for guidance.

**How are permit applications evaluated?**

Applicants will be contacted for clarification or if applications are incomplete within thirty (30) calendar days of receipt of the application package. If a sanctuary requests such additional information or clarification, and no response has been received from the applicant within ninety (90) calendar days, the application will be deemed withdrawn, no further action will be taken on the application, and any application for this activity will have to be resubmitted by the applicant as a new request.

Complete applications are reviewed by ONMS program officials, on-site sanctuary personnel, and, when deemed necessary, peer-reviewed by outside experts. As described in more detail in the policy and permit guidelines for submarine cable projects, applications will be judged on the basis of:

1.  The applicant's professional qualifications to conduct and complete the proposed activity;
2.  The adequacy of the applicant's financial resources available to conduct and complete the proposed activity;
3.  The duration of the proposed activity relative to its stated purpose;
4.  The methods and procedures proposed by the applicant in relation to the activity's impacts on sanctuary resources and qualities;
5.  The compatibility of the proposed activity with the sanctuary's primary objective to protect sanctuary resources and qualities, including considering the extent to which the conduct of the activity may diminish or enhance sanctuary resources and qualities, any indirect, secondary or cumulative effects of the activity, and the duration of such effects;
6.  The necessity of conducting the proposed activity within the sanctuary to achieve its purposes; and
7.  The reasonably expected end value of the activity to the furtherance of sanctuary goals.

Based on the review of the application in light of these criteria, ONMS will approve or deny the permit. If approved, the ONMS will issue the permit. If denied, applicants are notified of the reason(s) for denial and informed of the appeal process.

**What terms and conditions will be included on a cable permit?**

Permits for cable projects will include any terms and conditions deemed necessary to adequately protect and manage sanctuary resources. The specific conditions will necessarily vary from project to project. A description of the elements of a cable project that are generally subject to terms and conditions are given in the policy and permit guidelines for submarine cable projects.

**What monitoring will take place of permitted cable activities?**

A permitted submarine cable project will be monitored during and after installation to ensure compliance with the conditions of the permit. ONMS and on-site sanctuary personnel may periodically assess work in progress by visiting the study location and observing any permitted activity or by reviewing any required reports. The discovery of any irregularities not in conformance with the permit shall be promptly reported and appropriate action shall be taken. Permits will include a provision that the terms and conditions governing the activity can be changed if deemed necessary by the ONMS to protect sanctuary resources as a result of monitoring results. In addition, ONMS may require monitoring of seabed recovery post installation.

**How do I extend, change, or renew a permit?**

Once a permit or authorization has been issued, changes can be made in the form of an amendment. Requests for amendments (e.g., requests to change the activity location or to extend the expiration date) must conform to the policy and permit guidelines for submarine cable projects. Persons desiring to continue permitted submarine cable activities in a sanctuary should reapply for an extension of the current permit at least ninety (90) calendar days before it expires, unless otherwise specified in a condition of the original permit. Reference to the original application may be given in lieu of a new application, provided the scope of work does not change significantly and any required reports pertinent to the original permit have been submitted to and approved by ONMS staff. *Note: requests for amendments not received within the time frame specified above are not guaranteed to be processed before the requested effective date. In addition, expired permits cannot be amended or renewed.*

**Reporting Burden**

Submittal of the information described in these guidelines is required to obtain a permit pursuant to ONMS regulations (15 CFR Part 922). This data is used to evaluate the potential benefits of the activity, determine whether the proposed methods will achieve the expected results, evaluate any environmental impacts, and determine if issuance of a permit is appropriate. It is through this evaluation that the ONMS is able to use permitting to allow otherwise prohibited activities while protecting sanctuary resources and qualities.

Applicants are requested to indicate any information that is considered proprietary business information. Such information is typically exempt from disclosure to anyone requesting information pursuant to the Freedom of Information Act (FOIA). NOAA will make all possible attempts to protect such proprietary information, consistent with all applicable FOIA exemptions found at 5 U.S.C. § 552(b). Typically exempt information includes trade secrets, commercial, and financial information (5 U.S.C. § 552(b)(4)). Personal information affecting an individual's privacy will also be kept confidential, consistent with 5 U.S.C. § 552(b)(6) and applicable law.

The public reporting burden for this collection of information is estimated to average 80 hours, including the time for reviewing instructions, searching existing data sources, gathering and maintaining the data needed, and completing and reviewing the collection of information. Send comments regarding this burden estimate or any other aspect of this collection of information, including suggestions for reducing this burden, to National Permit Coordinator, NOAA Office of

National Marine Sanctuaries, 1305 East-West Highway (N/ORM6), Silver Spring, Maryland, 20910.

Notwithstanding any other provision of law, no person is required to respond to, nor shall any person be subject to a penalty for failure to comply with, a collection of information subject to the requirements of the Paperwork Reduction Act, unless that collection of information displays a currently valid OMB Control Number.

### APPLICATION REQUIREMENTS

All applications to install and maintain submarine cables in national marine sanctuaries should include, at a minimum, the following information:

A. General Project Information:
1. Name of the sanctuary(s) in which the submarine cable will be located.
2. Title of the submarine cable project.
3. Project summary or abstract (of no more than 3000 characters) that includes a statement of the project's objectives, the methods to be used, and why it is necessary that the activity occur within the boundaries of a sanctuary.
4. Objectives. Clearly state the objectives of the submarine cable project. Also state how these objectives further research, education, and/or management objectives of the sanctuary in which the cable project is proposed.
5. Project Significance. Discuss how the installation of the submarine cable, as proposed, would enhance or contribute to improving the state of knowledge, use of the sanctuary or overall objectives of the Sanctuary Management Plan. Explain why the project should be performed in the sanctuary and the potential benefits to the sanctuary. For educational permits, explain the educational value of the project.
6. The project's duration (i.e., the time from installation to removal of materials).
7. Funding source for the project.

B. Applicant Information and Certification:
1. Name, address, telephone number, fax number, email address and organizational affiliation (if applicable) of the primary applicant;
2. Identification of those authorized by the applicant to represent the applicant in meetings or phone consultations with sanctuary staff.
3. Identification of those who should receive project-related correspondence from the sanctuary;
4. Identification of individuals who would be supervising project activities. Provide qualifications and evidence of their ability to perform and supervise project-related tasks. For key personnel and the primary applicant, provide a list of other submarine cable projects from the past and any information that shows the current status of each project.
5. Identification of all applicant agents and consultants, as known at the time of application, and their contact information.
6. Signature of applicant certifying the application package is complete and correct to the best of the applicant's knowledge.

C. Project Route Description:
1. Provide a location and vicinity map showing where the proposed cable route is located in relation to other regional features. Include sanctuary boundaries on the location map.
2. The entire proposed project route should be described and depicted on route maps, drawn to scale. Starting and ending locations shall be clearly described and illustrated, as well as any connections to other project cables. As appropriate, the exact location of proposed landing sites shall be shown on a map and described with regard to size, location, and existing use. Route maps shall show sanctuary boundaries and other jurisdictional boundaries.
3. Provide a description of any routes that should be considered in the NEPA analysis of alternatives. Describe routes that were considered and eliminated and why they were eliminated. Include a site plan and description of each alternative.
4. Describe rationale for selecting proposed route, including specific factors that were considered.
5. Describe and map other fiber optic cable lines, pipelines, and/or telephone cable lines located in the project route area.
6. Define the minimum distance of separation necessary between the proposed project and any existing cable, pipelines or other structures. Explain the rationale for maintaining the specified distance. Explain how conflicts with existing cables or other structures will be avoided.
7. Provide one full-scale set of maps or charts derived from side-scan sonar and sub-bottom profile surveys conducted for the proposed project. The maps should show bathymetry, seabed features and profile, and shallow geology (e.g., depth or thickness of sediment substrate).
8. A written report of the above survey results should be included describing the length and area (total disturbance due to installation) of cable crossing with regards to the following: (a) low relief rocky substrate, (b) medium to high relief rocky substrate, (c) all other substrate types and slope conditions.

D. Cable Installation, Maintenance and Removal Procedures
*General Requirements*
1. Provide a detailed description of all elements of construction and installation (including pre-construction activities), the timing of these elements, and the overall project installation timeline. Provide hours of operation for installation and construction activities when appropriate.
2. Provide data on the exact locations where the cable will be buried into the seabed, when the burial will occur, where the cable will be laid on the seafloor, and when the cable laying will occur.
3. Quantify the rate of cable installation for each installation technique (e.g., burial vs. laying cable on the seafloor). Identify cable size and width of cable corridor. Identify the number of proposed cable landings, borings, conduits, and cables.
4. Identify onshore facilities required and/or proposed for the cable and provide contact information for any landowners, as appropriate.

5. Describe the proposed installation methods, including the proposed cable laying and burial techniques for different areas or substrate types and cable crossings, target cable burial depth, and boring operations and locations.
6. Identify the organization(s) that will install the cable.
7. Define the method used to calculate cable burial depth, with regard to trawling hazards.

*Drilling/Boring Activities at Landing Sites*
8. If boring is required, provide a detailed drilling plan, including detailed specifications of the boring machine (e.g., maximum pulling and snubbing capabilities, directional survey methods and controls, and allowable bore deviation tolerances) and scheduling for boring. Provide a contingency plan in the event of accidental surface mud fractures or lost circulation events.
9. Describe the basis/criteria for selecting the proposed directional bore depth. Verify whether or not the proposed depth is based on the existing subsurface soil conditions at the bore locations. Confirm that the proposed depth is deep enough to avoid the potential risk of sea bottom rupture during boring operations.
10. Submit detailed specifications of the mud system, including safety measures and a listing of all activities to be used and copies of the Material Safety Data Sheet (MSDS) for the drilling fluids.
11. Describe the potential for sea bottom rupture during boring. Identify the risks, potential impacts, and contingency plans for inadvertent sea bottom rupture, including measures to prevent the release of drilling fluids into ocean waters.
12. Develop and submit a contingency plan, in the event boring activities are required to be suspended and a partially-completed bore hole abandoned.

*Vessel Operations*
13. Identify the vessel or type/class of vessel proposed to be involved in installation and/or construction operations.
14. Identify vessel ingress and egress routes for any areas where water depth is less than 2x loaded draft of any vessel.
15. Submit vessel anchoring plans, including plans for any dive support vessels, which include (1) maps of the proposed anchor spreads and anchor locations or offshore temporary mooring locations for each work vessel and (2) a description of the procedures to be employed to minimize seafloor impacts.
16. Provide a work plan for construction during adverse weather conditions (e.g., storms, high winds, high seas), which includes a critical operations and curtailment plan. The plan should define the limiting conditions of sea state, wind, or any other conditions that exceed the safe and effective operation of vessels and equipment or divers in the water. The plan shall identify the onsite person with authority to determine critical conditions and suspend work operations.

*Cable Burial Specifications*
17. Submit a report describing the degree to which the cable can be buried to target burial depth along the entire route. Identify the plow's limitations for penetrating ocean floor sediment (sand, silt, gravel, cobble, small rock, soft rock, and hard rock) and alternative burial/cable laying methods in locations where plow cannot be used.

18. Document how the cable will remain buried and what mechanisms are in place to ensure long-term burial.
19. Identify water depth and distance from shore for cable burial. Explain factors used to determine how far out the cable will be buried.
20. Define the area of disturbance related to project construction and cable burial.
21. Describe contingency plans for areas where the cable is not sufficiently buried or where the cable becomes exposed after presumed burial.

*Cable Maintenance, Repairs, and Removal*
22. Describe any planned project repair and maintenance activities, including routine inspections and maintenance of the cable.
23. Include an estimate of the frequency of cable faults, and a description of how emergency repairs would be made. Identify plans for periodic surveys and other activities proposed to monitor cable burial success and impact avoidance.
24. Describe the cable identification system used by the company to distinguish its cable from other cables.
25. Identify the expected project life of the proposed cable.
26. Describe plans and procedures for removing the cable by the end of the permit's duration. If planning to abandon the cable in place, give the rationale including an explanation as to why the cable cannot be removed.

E. Environmental and Human Use Impacts. The application should include an analysis of the anticipated environmental and human use impacts of the proposed activity and alternatives to the proposed activity. This analysis should include:
1. Identification of all natural resources that could be affected by project construction, installation, operation, and removal (including the spatial and temporal range of these resources) and a description/analysis of how the project will impact these resources. When endangered, threatened, or protected species are present, a detailed itemization of species, quantity, and sizes of individuals (as applicable) should also be provided.
2. Identification of existing human uses that could be affected by the project (including but not limited to commercial and recreational fisheries, commercial and recreational activities, and vessel traffic and operations) and a description/analysis of how the project will impact these uses.
3. A description of any submerged historical resources that may exist in the project area, including any sonar/magnetometer surveys or other data used to arrive at the conclusion, a description/analysis of the how might impact these resources, and any proposed mitigations.
4. Characterization of the benthic habitat to be affected by the project (including nearshore/landing areas, as applicable), and analysis of the impacts of the project on the biological resources of any affected habitat.
5. Analysis of the geology and geophysical characteristics of the project area, including sediment types, location of hard bottom and rocky substrate, and the presence of canyons, faults and other potentially unstable areas.
6. A description of if/how the proposed cable project will interact with other natural and human-caused impacts on natural and historical resources (e.g., cumulative effects).

7. An analysis of the environmental effects of each alternative. Note that, depending on the alternatives selected, these descriptions may be redundant with the description of the environmental consequences of the proposal.

F. Supporting Information:
1. Project Budget. Include a project budget for the proposed project, including cost estimates for construction, installation, operations, monitoring and removal. Indicate if different portions of the project are being funded by different sources. Prior to undertaking any permitted activities, the applicant will be required (as a condition of any permit) to show proof of a performance bond or equivalent financial assurance to cover certain costs (including cable monitoring and removal) in the event the applicant is not able to fund or conduct any activities as required by the permit. This proof may be, but is not required to be, submitted at the time of permit application.

2. Surveys and other data. Include a summary of all surveys and studies conducted for the proposed project to date. These should include methods, geographic area covered, transect locations, and any associated photographs/video. In addition, copies of any ROV video, side scan sonar, or other survey data collected to date that may assist in determining both the current environmental state of the project area as well as potential impacts should be included. The office may request that full survey data be provided based on review of summary information.

3. Other permits:
a. Submit a list of all federal, state, and local licenses, permits, or other authorizations required to install and operate the submarine cable. Provide copies of those obtained and status of those pending.
b. Identify the status of the project with the U.S. Army Corps of Engineers, National Marine Fisheries Service (NOAA Fisheries), U.S. Fish and Wildlife Service, and any other Federal, state, or local authority whose permit, authorization, or approval is required.

## Permit Application Terms and Conditions

In addition to the application requirements listed above, permits for submarine cable projects may include additional terms and conditions deemed necessary to adequately protect and manage sanctuary resources. These conditions may include, but are not limited to, the following:

1. Cable installation requirements and procedures, including the entity and vessel-type to conduct the installation, NOAA observer coverage, weather restrictions, required cable burial depth, specifications for burial in different seabed types, prohibition on cable loops, and speed restrictions for vessel operations.
2. Any pre-installation survey requirements, such as pre-lay multi-beam sonar and grapple runs along the cable route.
3. Details of any monitoring or mitigation plans determined necessary to protect sanctuary resources and qualities, including required elements, schedules, and notifications;

4. Spill control measures, including development of a spill prevention and control and countermeasure plan ("spill plan") and a drill fluid monitoring and remediation plan for any horizontal directional drilling activities.

5. Archeological resources assessment and procedures, including review of the cable corridor for historical resources and procedures to be followed if archeological resources are discovered during the conduct of permitted activities.

6. Any required notifications to affected sanctuary offices and other personnel or agencies.

7. Vessel operations requirements, including procedures for notification of vessels and the US Coast Guard of permitted activities, mitigations required to minimize marine bird collisions due to project lighting, and regulations of vessel discharge.

8. Any required coordination with fishermen or fishing organizations affected by the cable project, which may include fishermen reimbursement.

9. Procedures to be taken in event of a marine mammal or fishing gear entanglement;

10. Requirement for certain post-lay inspection and burial surveys, data, and reports, which may include a Post-Lay Inspection and Burial (PLIB) survey, raw georeferenced data from the PLIB survey, PLIB report from the survey, and updated charts.

11. When the permitted activities include placement of scientific equipment, requirements for requests for new equipment as well as procedures governing the removal and retrieval of equipment.

12. Development and implementation of cable monitoring and survey plans covering the life of the cable, to include survey types, frequency, ROV and observer coverage, cable tracking system technology requirements, mitigation measures in case of unanticipated impacts to sanctuary resources, and a cable reburial plan.

13. Cable repair procedures, including any required plans, notifications, approvals, and post-repair reports.

14. Procedures governing removal of the cable, including development and approval of a cable removal plan.

15. Bonding and insurance requirements covering the conduct of activities under the permit, to include any required monitoring or removal of the cable and associated structures.

16. For cable projects authorized under special use permits, the amounts and payment schedule for fees associated with processing and administering the permit as well as the fair market value of the use of sanctuary resources.

www.ingramcontent.com/pod-product-compliance
Lightning Source LLC
Chambersburg PA
CBHW080351290526
45791CB00009BA/2834